For Blake
Warm regards
Ellen Sue
Stern

Y0-BQX-628

Words of

Inspiration

For

People

With

MS

Ellen Sue Stern

*Dedicated with gratitude to the courageous
individuals with MS around the world who have
inspired this work and to the medical and scientific
community involved in the effort to find a cure.*

Copyright © 2005 Ellen Sue Stern

All rights reserved. No part of this book may be reproduced
or transmitted in any form or by any means, electronic or
mechanical, including photocopying, recording, or using any
information storage and retrieval system, without written
permission from the publisher, except in the case of brief
quotations embodied in critical articles and reviews.

Distributed by
Itasca Books
5120 Cedar Lake Road
Minneapolis, MN 55416

Printed in the United States of America

ISBN 0-9767054-0-0

Interior Design by Tamara J.M. Peterson

Cover Art by Scott Norris
Scott Norris is a long-term brain cancer survivor. Through his
journey of recovery, he has developed a deeper appreciation
for the richness and vibrancy of life. See Scott's work at
http://www.home.earthlink.net/~norbird/

To order additional copies of this book go to
www.itascabooks.com or www.ellensuestern.com

The first in a series of WORDS OF INSPIRATION Books for
people with chronic conditions and their carepartners.

ENDORSEMENTS

"*Words of Inspiration For People with MS* gives us just what we need to live life with MS with hope, perspective, and resolve. Thanks to Ellen Sue, we now have a handbook filled with soulful inspiration, practical tips, and powerful affirmations giving us the tools to move forward, no matter what challenges lie ahead. WORDS OF INSPIRATION is one of those books that we will carry with us everywhere; one of those books that will become a precious worn treasure."
    –Jackie Waldman, Author Courage to Give Series

"In my many years of working with multiple sclerosis I have read many inspirational books written by many well-intentioned individuals. Ellen Sue Stern's is clearly among the best! She looks with feeling from the inside out and does it with a soft and objective, very honest point of view. It is inspiring, easy to read and very educational. I highly recommend this book for all associated with multiple sclerosis, professional as well as personal."
    –Randall T. Schapiro, M.D. The Schapiro Center for Multiple Sclerosis at the Minneapolis Clinic of Neurology

"*Words of Inspiration for people with MS* is a godsend. I found myself filled with emotions I didn't even know I had while reading this "very necessary" book for those living with MS. Life is a party, Elle! Thanks for the invite!"
    –Jackie S. Bertone, Film & Recording Industry Percussionist, living with MS since 1996

"Ellen Sue Stern's *Words of Inspiration* offers exactly what the title implies. Page after page brings uplifting and profound messages of courage and hope that point to brighter days. Stern masterfully combines inspirational quotes and affirmations with the all too familiar reality of living with MS. *Words of Inspiration for People With MS* brought me empowerment, joy and the ability to view MS as a blessing in my life."

–*Kristie Salerno Kent*, District Marketing Manager for Borders Group Inc. and Living with MS since 1999.

"*Words of Inspiration for People with MS* is a book to carry with you through out your own journey in life. Whenever you encounter a bump in the road or a new path, this book will help you gain strength to move forward. Ellen Sue offers hope and inspiration and lets us know that we are not alone. Thank you Ellen Sue."

–*Amelia Davis*, Photographer and author of My Story: A Photographic Essay On Life With Multiple Sclerosis.

"Ellen Sue Stern's book is inspiring and uplifting. Her spirit shines through and her message rings true for people with MS and the people who love them."

–*Maureen Reeder,* President, National MS Society, Minnesota Chapter

INTRODUCTION

I've had MS half my life. I've had a diagnosis for almost three years. And now, I'm finallyready to write about it.

Albert Einstein said: God doesn't roll dice with the universe. Or as I like to say: What we're given is our fate, what we do with it is our destiny. The Latin word for destiny is determination. Moment by moment, day by day, we shape our own destiny, fueled by the determination to take action on our own behalf.

Like everyone living with MS, I have good days and bad days. For me, being absorbed in work helps a lot. So does humor. Prayer. Shopping. But what helps the most is my unwavering conviction that things happen for a reason. Writing books is my way of turning lemons into lemonade; of discovering the proverbial "silever linings" which always reveal themselves when we're open to the grand adventure of life, in all its joy and adversity.

We share the challenge of living with MS, but our symptoms, what inner and outer resources we call on to deal with them, bears the unique stamp of our individuality. What works for me may or may not work for you. But I promise you this: Having MS changes us. *GROWS* us. Makes us stronger, better, more powerful and loving human beings.

Ultimately, what counts are our best intentions and our commitment to stay the course. Writing this book has been a heartwarming experience and yet another exercise in pushing through what, at times, seemed like insurmountable odds. A three-month relapse forced me to push back deadlines, and much of the writing was done in ten to twenty hour marathons, glued to the computer, when I was unbelievably exhausted. Yet it was important for me to complete one more "chapter" in the yet unwritten memoir. Along the way, I've met all sorts of amazing people living with MS. I've been moved by their stories—proud to be a member of this global family of fighters—and we are fighters, my friends, each and every one of us. And so I thank you for inspiring me to keep going as I offer you these words: Wherever the road leads, may you be blessed with peace.

Ellen Sue Stern

A portion ot the proceeds of this book will be contributed to the National MS Society and other worthy causes supporting people living with MS.

DIAGNOSIS

Long afterwards, she was to
remember that moment when her
life changed its direction.

Evelyn Anthony

Each of us has our Diagnosis Story—the pivotal moment when we were told we definitely had MS. For some of us it took years of painful tests, running from doctor to doctor, desperately trying to figure out what was wrong; these days, improved technology and the emergence of better diagnostic tools makes it possible to get a definitive answer within weeks, sometimes even days after symptoms appear.

Whether it took forever or came as sudden, startling news, finding out we have MS has a profound impact. Our initial reaction may have been shock or disbelief; we may have felt scared, angry, hopeless, overwhelmed, even relieved to finally know what was wrong.

The realities of living with MS sink in gradually, over time. But the moment of diagnosis becomes a turning point in our history.

AFFIRMATION: I REMEMBER

INSTABILITY

Sit, walk, or run.
But don't wobble.

Zen proverb

We all have our "wobbly" days, days when, no matter how hard we try to stay on firm ground, any one of many balance related MS symptoms causes us to lose our footing. One leg goes numb and we're suddenly in a heap on the floor. Vertigo makes the room spin around in a dizzying and disorienting roller coaster ride. We lean more heavily on our cane; we have to steady ourselves before attempting the handicapped accessible ramp.

And then there are the emotional tremors, the fear and anxiety that challenge our capacity to remain calm. What can we hang on to when everything seems so shaky? How do we get a grip—literally and figuratively—when life seems anything but stable?

Wobbly doesn't mean weak; it takes tremendous resolve to maintain both physical and emotional composure. We may sit in a wheelchair. We may walk with a limp, but as long as we stay true to our inner compass we have what it takes to stay the course.

AFFIRMATION: I AM SECURE IN MY CORE.

KINDNESS

My religion is very simple—
my religion is kindness.

His Holiness the Dalai Lama

Why is it that people are more inclined to offer kindness in times of sickness and crisis? A friend we've lost touch with lands in the hospital and we go out of our way to send flowers. Personal grudges and family tensions get tabled when someone we love is in trouble.

Witnessing pain makes us more acutely aware of our own vulnerability; we can't help but think: "there but for the grace of God go I." But we needn't reserve acts of kindness for emergencies. Being kind, not only to others, but also toward ourselves, is powerfully healing. By softening our heart, we let go of harsh judgments in favor of accepting ourselves—and others—as perfectly imperfect human beings, helping one-another in a spirit of compassion.

AFFIRMATION: KINDNESS IS CONTAGIOUS.

OPTIMISM

There is one thing that gives
radiance to everything. It is the idea
of something around the corner.

C.K. Chesterton

We read, surf the net, and talk to our doctors to find out the latest developments in MS research. We cross our fingers and our toes as we slide (or is it glide?) through the silver tube, praying for an improved, or at least, stable MRI. A bgzillion dollars are being spent on research by the best and the brightest doctors and scientists around the world.

I know, I know. We can send a man to the Moon, so why can't we grow myelin? Yet, look how far we've come with the emergence of disease modifying drugs. Handicapped access. The very fact that I can sit at my computer at 2:30 am in Minneapolis, knowing I can call a 24 hour MS help line or sign on to a website and share MS stories with someone in Slovenia is mind-blowing, to say the least.

We don't have all the answers, but we're making strides, quantum leaps, really, in the global effort to understand and cure—yes, cure—MS.

AFFIRMATION: I AM OPTIMISTIC ABOUT THE FUTURE.

SILVER LININGS

People who have not been in Narnia
sometimes think that a thing cannot be good
and terrible at the same time.

C.S. Lewis

People with MS have an amazing capacity to see the cup as half full: Our legs are numb, but we're still ambulatory. We're in a wheelchair, but we still have our sight. Our sight is dimmed, but we've made all sorts of friends who admire our seeing eye dog.

Sometimes it's a reach. No one can constantly maintain a positive attitude. It takes enormous faith to believe there is goodness, perhaps even greatness within the not-so-great hand we've been dealt.

If today is one of those days when you're open to seeing the positives, consider the wonderful things that have come your way since being diagnosed with MS: The support you've received. The courage you've displayed. The surprising moments when you've said to yourself: I would never be who I am today, were it not for the challenges of living with MS. If today is one of those not-so-great days, know that tomorrow is another day, another opportunity to see the silver linings,

AFFIRMATION: I HAVE FAITH IN MY ABILITY TO SEE THE SILVER LININGS.

DECISIVENESS

Try? There is no try.
There is only do or not do.

Yoda

The first time I ever heard this quote was from a dear friend who had learned the difference between "trying" and "doing" in a chemical dependency treatment program. I bristled at the idea; after all, shouldn't people get gold stars for effort?

Now I understand, especially since I've realized that this concept has served me well in facing pressing decisions related to living with MS, for example, Am I willing and ready to begin taking a disease modifying drug? Should I start writing a new book or not, since who knows whether I'll be well enough to finish it?

Some choices have more far-reaching implications; some appear more mundane, but are equally critical, like: Should I get out of bed this morning?—not *try* to get out of bed, but *get* out of bed!

Making a choice—and then choosing our choice with confidence and commitment is a powerful stance. Trying is commendable. But ultimately, *doing* is how we manifest real change in our lives.

AFFIRMATION: I WILL ACT WITH CONVICTION.

TENACITY

I pulled out the old, red Encyclopedia Britannica
from the 1970's, brushed off years of dust and
looked under Multiple Sclerosis. It read:
"A debilitating and degenerative
disease resulting in paralysis."

Kari Bertch

Imagine reading these chilling words at the tender age of 19: the abysmal prognosis would have been enough to make anyone throw in the towel. But not Kari Bertch—a lovely, resilient woman who, some twenty years later, is anticipating the birth of her first child.

I shudder at what may have happened if Kari, along with so many people who were given this stark and dismal description of MS before we knew what we know today, would have accepted a life-sentence as invalids on an inevitable downward spiral toward paralysis. Yet another example of the human spirit at its finest, refusing to give up, defying the odds, believing in ourselves instead of allowing the so-called "facts" to define who we are and what we're capable of accomplishing.

Today's definition may well become tomorrow's footnote as our understanding of MS continues to unfold.

AFFIRMATION: MY STORY IS STILL BEING WRITTEN

PREJUDICE

Woman with no limbs sues Air France.
Associated Press—August 13TH, 2004

This headline was so outrageous; at first I thought it was something out of the nationally syndicated column, News of the Weird. Not so. According to several news accounts, an Air France employee in Manchester told the woman, Adele Price, 42: "One head, one bottom and a torso cannot possibly fly on its own". The story quickly became fodder for late night comedy with jokes like: "It'll get thrown out of court; she doesn't have a leg to stand on." And "My response would have been "that's why I'm taking a plane you moron."

Giving Air France the benefit of the doubt, i.e. safety concerns, this story highlights the issue of discrimination against people who are disabled, in the workplace, in public venues, and in countless subtle and not so subtle stereotypes and slights. We are fortunate to live in a time and place in which there is sensitivity and accommodation for individuals with special needs. But we still have a long way to go. We must fight prejudice and advocate for human rights— not just for those of us living with MS, but for all people, everywhere.

AFFIRMATION: I WILL STAND UP TO PROTECT
THE DIGNITY AND HUMAN RIGHTS OF PEOPLE
WITH DISABILITIES.

PATIENCE

Have patience with all things,
but first of all with yourself.

St. Francis of Sales

How to be patient while praying for a remission, knowing we have little, if any, control over the situation? How to be patient with symptoms that limit our ability to do the things that make us feel useful and give meaning to our lives?

Whether its meeting work deadlines, cleaning the house, playing with our children or making time for friends, living with MS forces us to constantly adjust our expectations of ourselves.

It's easy to say, "alter your expectations", but lowering the bar doesn't exactly enhance our self-image or motivate us to keep going. On the other hand, forcing ourselves to take on too much is a sure recipe for frustration and exhaustion. My personal compromise is to push myself when I'm feeling relatively well so that I'm ahead of the game if and when I'm flattened again. Then I gently remind myself:

AFFIRMATION: I'M DOING THE BEST I CAN

OPPORTUNITY

Life is full of obstacle illusions.

Grant Frazier

Upon learning he has MS, a confirmed workaholic commits to spending more time with his family. A depressed, overweight woman with a sedentary secretarial job gets serious about her health. A 30-year-old mother of three fulfills her lifelong passion of becoming a painter.

Recognizing opportunities in the midst of crisis requires identifying the ways in which seeming obstacles are, indeed, openings for transformation. One person living with MS might have the proverbial "ah hah!" experience that inspires a profound commitment to make positive strides toward personal growth; others might make smaller, but equally significant changes, like starting to exercise or improving their diet.

Living with MS can be a unique opportunity to learn and grow. Opportunities abound. But only when we are ready to identify and act on them.

AFFIRMATION: WHAT AM I LEARNING?

RAGE

I have decided to stick with love.
Hate is too great a burden to bear.

Martin Luther King, Jr.

We only have so much energy—why waste it on hate when love is infinitely more rewarding? Hatred saps our precious life power and diminishes who we are; being loving infuses us with energy and makes us more capable of being our best, most divine selves.

None of which discounts the real, raw feelings of rage we may grapple with. After my son, Evan, was diagnosed with bi-polar disorder, we talked about how hard it was to accept his diagnosis. He said: "I'm just not ready to embrace this." Why in the world would you think you have to embrace this? I asked. His answer: "Because you've embraced having MS."

For the record: I hate having MS. That said, I love the ways in which am learning to live with it, and, more importantly, how much I give myself credit—how much I give all of us credit—for overcoming bitterness in favor of love.

AFFIRMATION: I CHOOSE LOVE

TEARS

Rich tears!
What power lies in
those falling drops!

Mary Delarivier Manley

Each of us expresses feelings in our own way. Depending on our upbringing, we may associate crying with inconsolable loss reserved for only the most devastating disasters, like finding out someone we love is terminally ill. Terrible accidents. Terrorist attacks. Death.

Some people cry at the drop of a hat; others are more stoic. There are people who relish a good cry and others who dread the possibility of breaking down in tears. Personally, I can't rave enough about the healing power of tears, but then again, I've been known to weep reading obituaries of people I've never even met.

Sobbing can be a wonderful release—the emotional equivalent of a thunderstorm followed by a deep, cleansing calm and renewed energy to face what comes.

AFFIRMATION: SOMETIMES IT HELPS TO HAVE A GOOD CRY.

RESILIENCY

There is often in people to whom
"the worst" has happened an almost
transcendent freedom, for they have
faced "the worst" and survived it.

Carol Pearson

We see it all the time. The eerily angelic photograph of a child with leukemia in People Magazine. An inspirational speaker whose words ring with truth in describing a near brush with death. My 84 year-old father's calm, reassuring presence, walking around with only one artery open, knowing any moment may be his last.

Likewise, many of us living with MS feel a certain sense of peacefulness and freedom as a result of continuing to survive-and thrive-despite enormous pain and adversity. New symptoms are less upsetting once we realize how capable we are of coping with them. Living with the unknown doesn't seem quite so ominous as we learn to stay focused in the present and confident that we have what it takes to carry on. We may or may not have seen the worst—but we know who we are and we know what we're made of, which makes all the difference in the world.

AFFIRMATION: EVERYTHING WILL BE ALL RIGHT

WORKPLACE

*I was beginning to appreciate how
truly difficult I was making life for the people
I worked with, the majority of whom didn't know
about my health issues. My behavior must
have seemed flaky at best....*

Michael J. Fox

In his memoir, Lucky Man, actor Michael J. Fox,
describes the craziness he felt before going public with
the news of his Parkinson's.

While most of us don't share his celebrity status,
we still face the dilemma of deciding if, when, and
how to disclose that we have MS. Regardless of a
company's official policies, we may fear the more
subtle discrimination that can accompany the stigma
of having a serious, chronic disease, such as our
co-workers looking at us differently. Being passed over
for a promotion. Losing our job, and worse yet, our
health insurance.

Being forthcoming about living with MS can be risky
business or an incredible relief. Worst-case scenario,
we may feel more vulnerable in the workplace; best-
case scenario, we may be pleasantly surprised by the
outpouring of support from our colleagues.

AFFIRMATION: I NEEDN'T LET MS GET IN THE WAY OF
MY CAREER.

STEREOTYPES

I am not deaf, I thought to myself.
I am still not sure why people raise their
voices when talking to someone
in a cast or a wheelchair.

Frank Boehm, M. D.

It's a strange phenomenon, one I see at the nursing home where my mother is wheelchair bound with infarct dementia. She can't walk, she can't dress herself, and she isn't much of a conversationalist, but there's absolutely nothing wrong with her hearing! However irrational, we may think that if we just talk loudly enough, she'll understand what we're saying and maybe even say something lucid, like: "Why are you screaming?!? I can hear just fine!"

Its common to talk down to people with disabilities and to make all sorts of assumptions, including the mistaken belief that everyone with MS is in a continual state of deterioration or that people with MS shouldn't have children or that people in wheelchairs are likely to also be blind, deaf, brain damaged, or God knows, what else?

Bottom line: Living with MS increases our sensitivity to stereotypes. How to respond:

AFFIRMATION: EDUCATE! EDUCATE! EDUCATE!

CALCULATED RISKS

Please know that I am aware of the hazards.
I want to do it because I must do it.

Amelia Earhart

In his book, BLINDSIGHTED: A RELUCTANT MEMOIR, journalist and MS patient, Richard Cohen, describes his insistence on taking subways instead of cabs and stairs instead of elevators. His wife, television personality, Meredith Viera, says: "I hate it. I think he sometimes puts his life in danger and it worries me."

I'd worry, too. There's a fine line between empowering ourselves and endangering ourselves. Some risks are worth taking because they enhance our sense of mastery and independence. Others may be dangerous, self-destructive or just plain stupid! We may need to test ourselves, but we mustn't fall into the trap of ignoring common sense to prove anything to anyone. We take responsibility for our actions, measuring the risks and taking our loved ones' feelings into consideration. At the end of the day, we must know that we've done all we can, putting it all out there without pushing ourselves to the point of diminishing returns.

AFFIRMATION: I WILL THINK TWICE BEFORE TAKING RISKS.

VISION

*Just because a man loses the use of his eyes
doesn't mean he lacks vision.*

Stevie Wonder

Optic neuritis is a fairly common MS symptom, in many cases the first clue that something is wrong. On the positive side, the dramatic onset of vision problems tends to be relatively short lived and/or reversible. Even so, lots of people with MS experience marked deterioration in vision, yet another example of a loss that requires a choice between falling into despair and finding a way to "see" things in a different light.

Without sugarcoating, it helps to remember the distinction between sight and vision. Sight is external, vision comes from within. Sight is limited; vision knows no bounds. Having never experienced blindness, I can't imagine how difficult it must be. But I know this much: We can be blind and still have vision, the core of all creativity, the inner eye that fashions our view of the world and guides us forward in our path.

AFFIRMATION: I HAVE INFINITE VISION.

DEPRESSION

I'm not going to lie down
and let trouble walk over me.

Ellen Glasgow

Sometimes it's fine to curl up under the covers and sometimes we need to fight! Putting up a good fight can be critically important—even life-saving—especially if we're struggling with depression, which can be part and parcel of living with MS.

There are plenty of good reasons to feel defeated when the disease process brings new and/or worsening symptoms that compromise the quality of our lives, diminishing mobility, robbing us of our independence, threatening our self-image or wreaking havoc with our relationships.

Considerable numbers of people with MS suffer bouts of depression; fortunately, there are myriad resources available. Despair can be an emotionally healthy reaction to living with MS, but if it becomes a chronic, paralyzing demon, its time to seek professional help. Talk to someone you trust. Make an appointment with your medical provider and place your faith in the promise that your life—MS and all—is well worth fighting for.

AFFIRMATION: I WILL REACH OUT FOR HELP

UNSOLICITED SYMPATHY

I know exactly how you feel.
Lots of well-meaning, but terribly annoying people

What is it about these words that make us feel like screaming: "No. You don't know how I feel. In fact, you don't even have a clue!" Try, for example, explaining MS-related fatigue to someone who needs a good night's rest. Or describing the constant sensation of pins and needles, feeling like you're burning up when your temperature is normal, restless leg syndrome, vertigo, incontinence, and any number of other physical challenges (and indignities) of living with MS, not to mention the significant economic and emotional toll it can take.

No wonder we feel enraged at the sheer presumption that anyone, regardless of his or her best intentions, can truly understand what its like to live with MS. That said, there's no excuse for rude retorts. However clumsy, people are just trying to help. Embrace the intention. Let go of the rest.

AFFIRMATION: IT'S NOT WORTH GETTING UPSET OVER

SUPPORT

There was only one thing we had in common:
none of us wanted to be there.

Xenia Rose

It's a good start! Whether it's signing up for an early diagnosis support group, attending an MS patient program, or participating in a walkathon, none of us would have eagerly signed up for membership in this particular club.

Yet doing so can be a real lifesaver. Some of us seize the opportunity to attend a support group, grateful for the empathy and information that only comes from having "been there"—a quality even the most devoted friends can't necessarily offer. On the other hand, we may be put off by the idea of spilling our guts to utter strangers, much less being burdened by their grief.

Getting involved in a support group, whether you're ready now or considering it down the line—is a personal choice with some very tangible perks: It's a great way to meet people who relate to what we're going through. It's a terrific resource for learning coping strategies direct from the front line. And, it's a way of getting perspective. As we get to know others in various stages of living with MS, we are more able to assess our own growth and healing.

AFFIRMATION: SUPPORT IS GOOD, IN WHATEVER FORM FEELS RIGHT.

COGNITIVE PROBLEMS

*You may forget your keys, misplace
your wallet, drop a glass or misspell your
own name—several times in a row.*

Harold Bloomfield

"I kept joking that I had early Alzheimer's, but deep down I was really scared I was losing it," says Jill, a recently diagnosed schoolteacher. "Fortunately, I had read about cognitive problems associated with MS; still, it was frightening to feel as if I was losing my mind."

Memory loss, mental distraction and disorientation are cognitive issues faced by a fair share of individuals living with MS, so here are some anxiety-reducing memory aids: 1. Always keep your keys, wallet, and other valuables in the same place. 2. Make lists (phone number lists, grocery lists, to do lists) instead of relying on memory. 3. Tell someone where you put the lists in case you forget.

Most importantly, don't panic! Focus on one thing at a time-it's the best way to keep your head on straight enough to handle everything you're dealing with right now.

AFFIRMATION: THE AUTHOR HAS BEEN WRITING ALL NIGHT AND IS IN A MS MENTAL MELTDOWN, SO GO AHEAD AND MAKE UP ONE YOURSELF.

VULNERABILITY

The word courage derives from coeur,
the French word for "heart."

John Welwood

I like this definition; it implies a softening of our heart rather than a hardening of will in order to survive.

It's common for people to think that courage is a matter of squaring our shoulders and pushing through our pain. In fact, vulnerability is the prerequisite to courage. Bravery in the face of adversity is measured by our willingness to transcend bravado for the far more difficult task of allowing our sadness to surface, our fears to be exposed (and that means, you, too, all you MS alpha males out there!)

Even as we go on with our daily lives, we pray for the courage to let our hearts lead the way, to feel the full measure of what living with MS means in our lives.

AFFIRMATION: I AM BRAVE ENOUGH TO LET MY HEART CRACK OPEN.

DENIAL

If we are coping magnificently,
shedding no tears and carrying on as
if nothing has happened, we are
only deceiving ourselves.

Judith Viorst

We may feel pressured to hold ourselves together for others' sake, or put ourselves on autopilot as protection against experiencing the full brunt of our feelings, which, if unleashed, seem like an uncontrollable torrent that will sweep us under, rendering us incapable of getting through the day.

Coping—carrying on as if its business as usual—has been drummed into us-and naturally, there are times when we need to be circumspect about when, how, and with whom to share our feelings. But putting up a good front ultimately complicates the healing process. We must give ourselves permission to remove our façade, let down and let go of our need to stay strong. Real strength returns when we feel safe to feel and share what's really going on inside.

AFFIRMATION: IT'S OK TO ACT AS IF EVERYTHING ISN'T OK, EVERY MINUTE OF EVERY DAY.

HOPE

Hope is the feeling that the feeling
you have isn't permanent.

Jean Kerr

If I were to choose just one quote to put on my wall, it would likely be this one.

It suggests that hope is what ultimately gets us through even the most dreadful experiences, including serious MS relapses and/or new and escalating symptoms. It affirms that our feelings of hopelessness—and who doesn't feel hopeless once in a while?—are a normal response to living with MS. And, it reminds us that our despondency is temporary—a positive promise to hold on to when we fear that pain is our permanent destiny.

Time and time again I've heard people with MS say: "The one thing that's kept me going is believing that I won't always feel this way." Feelings ebb and flow, changing subtly all the time. Tomorrow will be better than today-and the next day and the next. I will hold on to hope and remember that:

AFFIRMATION: CHANGE IS THE ONLY THING WE CAN TRULY COUNT ON.

HOLIDAYS

hol·i·day (noun)
2. A day of exemption from labor;
a day of amusement and gayety.
Webster's Revised Unabridged Dictionary

Celebrating holidays can be heartwarming, nerve-wracking, or a combination of both. Try navigating a wheelchair through a crowded mall of hysterical last minute shoppers. Or timing a turkey just right, so that you're not napping when its thermometer pops out. Or giving generously when disability has put a dent in an already thin-stretched budget.

Perfectly healthy individuals get overwhelmed by preparing traditional meals, attending work parties, dealing with family dynamics, and giving the perfect gifts. Factor in MS and the stress level shoots right off the chart.

When we lose sight of the real meaning of holidays—marking passages, honoring rituals, expressing our love to one another—we miss out on so much. And, if we're not careful, we jeopardize our health. The great thing about holidays is that each year brings a new opportunity to do it right. By pacing ourselves. By preparing in advance. And, most importantly, by creating an experience of gratitude and joy.

AFFIRMATION: I WILL CHERISH THE TRUE MEANING OF HOLIDAYS.

INTIMACY ISSUES

I asked if he was afraid of catching MS from me.
He didn't have to answer.

Betty Cuthber, Three Time Gold Medal Winner

Betty Guthber, marathon sprinter, best known as Australia's "Golden Girl", could outrun just about anyone in the world. But when she shared her MS diagnosis with the man she loved, he couldn't run away fast enough, as she describes in her autobiography: "From then on he walked about six paces ahead of me everywhere we went and wouldn't come near me. It took a long time for me to get over him."

Living with MS tests our most intimate relationships. Some partners join forces, their foundation strengthened by the shared commitment to see it through. Others fold. Although the divorce rate is the same as in the general population, the pressure of living with MS can be the "tipping point"—the last straw in an already shaky relationship, be it marriage or any other intimate partnership.

If this pertains to you, know that you are not alone. And, know that it will get better. Not all at once, but over time you will heal and love again.

AFFIRMATION: THIS HURTS.

HUMOR

My first neurologist had a very holistic
approach to the illness. No more red meat,
no more salt, no more alcohol. I said, 'What
about sex?' He said, 'I'm seeing someone.'

Jonathan Katz

There's a definite case to be made for the healing properties of humor. In fact, scientific research has offered up some pretty impressive data when it comes to showing how laughter can be the best medicine, or at the very least, a serious component in the treatment of cancer, chronic illness, and certainly some of the pain and depression experienced by people with MS.

Releasing intense emotion, whether through laughter or tears, has a profound, cleansing effect that shifts our energy, boosts both our spirit and, quite possibly, our immune system. Laughter helps put things in perspective; when Katz, jokes: "I had a spinal tap, which didn't hurt. I had an MRI, where they put you in tube [for] 45 minutes, and I actually enjoyed the privacy" we realize again, that we aren't alone. Being able to laugh doesn't trivialize the tough stuff; it just makes it a little easier to deal with.

AFFIRMATION: I WILL SHARE THESE JOKES WITH SOMEONE ELSE WHO HAS MS SO THAT WE CAN LAUGH TOGETHER.

PARENTING

My mother was about twelve when she
stopped being able to lift the teapot.

J.K Rowling

...and only 45 when she died, which motivated her daughter, J.K.Rowling, world-famous author of the *Harry Potter* series, to become an outspoken advocate for people with MS.

It's hard being a parent living with MS. We don't want to appear vulnerable or helpless in our children's eyes. We hate having them see us suffer, we lose sleep over our ability to provide for them, we may even worry about them being embarrassed of us, wishing we were 'normal" like other parents they know.

On the bright side (yes, even this has a silver lining), our children's lives are enhanced by understanding that life isn't always easy. They become more self-reliant, and hopefully, more compassionate as they eventually come to appreciate all the love and care that goes into being the very best parents anyone could hope for.

AFFIRMATION: MY CHILDREN ARE RESILIENT
AND ARE LEARNING VALUABLE LIFE LESSONS.

SPIRIT

I have a strong heart; I have a strong soul.
I just have a little bit of trouble with my right leg,

The late Senator, Paul Wellstone

In the short span between being diagnosed with MS and his tragic death in 2002, Senator Paul Wellstone inspired thousands of people with his calm, understated perspective, along with the passion and purpose he brought to every part of his life.

We benefit from his legacy. Whether championing the rights of people with disabilities or refusing to let MS derail his career, his indomitable spirit is a gentle reminder to focus on our strengths.

Acknowledging the ways in which we are fully functional, maybe even remarkable, keeps us going and enables us to transcend our limitations. Our bodies may not work perfectly, but they must be awfully strong to withstand the ravages of MS. Our hearts may ache, but they're beating like a metronome; our soul expands as we continue to strengthen our resolve.

AFFIRMATION: I'M GETTING STRONGER EVERY DAY.

CHOICE

It's choice—not chance—that
determines your destiny.

Jean Nidetch

None of us would choose to have MS. But we can
choose how to live with it. No matter how crooked
the road, how high the bridge, how deep the holes,
we always have choices. How do we choose to meet
our particular set of challenges? How do we handle
the physical pain limitations we're faced with? How
do we greet each day without giving in to the fear
that disease will win out, that tomorrow will bring
more, maybe different sorts of obstacles, without
allowing anger or fear or self-pity to rule?

We choose every belief, every act with utter
confidence that, for better and for worse, this is what
we have been given and this is what we will learn from,
grow from, become stronger and better, not in spite of,
but because of our MS. It's a lot to live with. But each
day presents us with the opportunity to make powerful
choices. Begin now:

AFFIRMATION: I CHOOSE TO SEE MY MS AS A
CHALLENGE, NOT A CURSE.

ANGER

Holding on to anger, resentment and hurt
only gives you tense muscles, a headache and
a sore jaw from clenching your teeth.
Joan Lunden, in *Healthy Living Magazine*

Each of us expresses anger in our own, unique fashion.
We may howl with rage, shake our fist at the universe,
shut down, turn against ourselves with self-pity or let
cynicism undermine our relationship with God or
whatever spiritual source we call on for support.

Anger is healthy as long as it doesn't prevent us
from loving others or ourselves. In fact, we *should* be
angry; having MS isn't fair—but then, life isn't fair.
Denying or repressing anger poisons our attitude and
erodes the quality of our lives; expressing anger is part
of the healing process, a necessary step on the path
toward acceptance.

AFFIRMATION: LET IT IN, LET IT OUT, LET IT GO.

INVISIBLE SYMPTOMS

Sometimes I feel like taking out my wallet
and saying: Here's a picture of my son, a picture
of my dog, and a picture of my MRI.

A woman in one of my workshops

"But you look great!" It's the "but" that gets me, in what, under normal circumstances, would be a compliment. Sometimes I have to bite my tongue, especially when my face is in crushing pain, my vision is blurry, my leg is asleep and I'm so tired I could fall dead asleep in the middle of writing this sentence.

Like lots of people with MS, my symptoms are invisible, which can be a mixed blessing. Our MS is so real and ever-present that it's impossible to describe, harder yet when we aren't wearing a "badge" of sorts that tips people off. Reciting a litany of complaints is counterproductive, but feeling dismissed can be equally frustrating.

We don't have to answer to anyone. Ultimately, we choose what we do and don't share with our loved ones. Strangers, on the other hand, don't deserve the personal details of our lives.

AFFIRMATION: I KNOW WHO I AM AND I KNOW WHAT I'M LIVING WITH.

BALANCE

We can be sure that the greatest hope
for maintaining equilibrium in the face of
any situation rests within ourselves.

Francis J. Braceland, *O Magazine*, April 2003

MS comes with a variety of symptoms that challenge our physical and emotional balance: Dragging a leg as we slowly make our way through a crowded room. Running to the bathroom every five minutes. Carrying syringes when we travel. Leaving the party before it's even started because we can't stay awake one second longer.

There are no easy words of encouragement on this one. What is, is. We can, however, cultivate an attitude that helps us keep our lives in balance. How? By keeping it real and keeping things in perspective. By finding the middle ground between acknowledging our limitations and keeping ourselves on solid, optimistic footing that keeps us on the right path, sure footed, always moving forward.

AFFIRMATION: I CANNOT BE SHAKEN.

COMPARISONS

Everyone is necessarily the
hero of his own life story.

John Bart

It's helpful and reassuring to learn about treatment options and it can be inspiring to see others with MS who seem to be thriving despite living with seemingly more serious symptoms. Where this gets tricky, even dangerous,
is when we say to ourselves, At least I'm not in a wheelchair or blind or incontinent, as if somehow our experience is invalidated by having a relatively less debilitating case.

Our experience is our experience. Being aware of how much "worse" it could be is no more helpful than being aware of how much "better" it could be, unless doing so increases our gratitude and motivates us to make informed choices to enhance our health.

Each of us deals with unique symptoms and our own particular challenges. We can sympathize and we can empathize, as long as it's not at our own expense.

AFFIRMATION: MY EXPERIENCE IS UNIQUE. I WILL HONOR IT.

ROLE MODELS

The first great gift we can bestow
on others is a good example.

Thomas More

Prior to my diagnosis, I knew three people with MS;
a woman my age with vision problems and vertigo, a
shirt tail relative in a wheelchair with a feeding tube;
and an old college friend, David Wexler, who I hadn't
seen in years until January 20th, 2003.

I was whining about how freezing it was outside, when
I saw David masterfully maneuvering his wheelchair up
an icy ramp in subzero weather to hear me speak at an
MS event. I was awed and terrified. Was this what I had
to look forward to? I couldn't in a million years imagine
being anywhere near so competent and gracious,
yet there he was, smiling and thanking me for a
wonderful presentation.

He was the one who deserved applause. I thanked
him—and continue to thank him—for being a source
of inspiration.

AFFIRMATION: ONE OF MY ROLE MODELS
IS _____.

SLEEP DISORDERS

Sleep fast. We need the pillows.

The Talmud

Many years ago, during a severe episode of insomnia, I wrote a book called YAWN: BEDTIME READING FOR INSOMNIACS, a collection of the most numbingly boring reading material imaginable, including the small print on the back of the Sweepstakes entry forms, President Clinton's grand jury testimony, tip tables, Practical Palmistry, a stain removal chart, Income Tax Instructions, and a detailed analysis of the stages of periodontal disease.

At the time, some seven years prior to being diagnosed, I had no idea that insomnia, restless leg syndrome, and a slew of sleep disorders are common symptom of MS. Since then, I've discovered a wonderfully whimsical world of insomniacs through a variety of internet web sites, including my personal favorite: www.msersonlinenightowls.com, filled with advice and encouragement for those of us who need more sleep, less sleep, can't sleep, or are losing sleep over not getting enough sleep, in which case, I can only suggest a hot bath, warm cocoa, and these two words:

AFFIRMATION: SLEEP TIGHT

WONDER

Sometimes I've believed as many as
six impossible things before breakfast.

Lewis Carroll. "Alice in Wonderland"

What are your beliefs in regard to your MS? Do you believe you've been dealt a lousy hand or do you see this as an opportunity to learn and grow? Do you believe you are doomed to get sicker or do you believe you may be "gifted" with a long, even permanent remission? Do you believe there's little, if any hope for the future or do you believe that someday there will be a cure?

Beliefs are incredibly powerful. Lots of studies point to a positive relationship between what we believe is possible and what comes to pass, for example, cancer patients whose tumors have been shown to diminish as a result of a positive mental mindset. We may as well stack the odds by believing in the so-called "impossible"; it can't hurt and, who knows, it might help. Sometimes life surprises us. Especially when we're willing to expect a miracle.

AFFIRMATION: TODAY I WILL BE OPEN TO SURPRISES.

SEXUALITY

I can remember when the air
was clean and sex was dirty.

George Burns

If it feels like it's been that long, rest assured, you're
not alone. Living with a chronic illness can affect our
sexuality and the quality of intimacy with our partner.

Our libido may be diminished due to meds or times
when we just plain aren't up to it (excuse the pun, guys.)
MS can also negatively impact our self-image. Thinking
of ourselves as sickly, dependent or disabled is no
aphrodisiac; it's hard (sorry, again) to feel sexy or
alluring when we're limping, drugged down, bleary-
eyed or suffering any other MS or meds-related
side effects.

Lovemaking is an essential part of an intimate
relationship. So is touching, holding, spooning and all
the other ways in which we express our sexual feelings
and desires. Sexuality falls into the category of things
that are good for us, make us feel good, and keep us
physically, emotionally, and spiritually nourished.

AFFIRMATION: I STILL WANT TO TOUCH AND
BE TOUCHED.

CONFIDENCE

If I have lost confidence in myself,
I have the universe against me.

Ralph Waldo Emerson

We're committed to our plan of therapy, but we
second-guess ourselves when we read about about
side effects. Our annual MRI appointment has us head
tripping every worst-case scenario. We've been in
remission for three and half years, when suddenly
we're obsessing about relapse.

No-one—and I mean *no-one*, feels secure all the time;
even if we have a rock solid foundation or the spiritual
faith of Mother Teresa, the idiosyncratic nature of MS
is bound to occasionally shake our confidence.

That's when we need to reach out and ask for
support from the Universe by focusing our energy on a
positive outcome. Finding a creative outlet through art,
prayer, ritual, nature or meditation can bolster our
confidence. It also doesn't hurt to "borrow" a little
confidence from our loved ones, medical providers or
other trusted members of our community. We diminish
our fear by dancing with forces far greater than ourselves.

AFFIRMATION: I HAVE CONFIDENCE IN THE HEALING
POWER OF THE UNIVERSE.

ASSERTIVENESS

*If there are no stupid questions, then what
kind of questions do stupid people ask? Do they
get smart just in time to ask questions?*

Scott Adams

It's not that we get "smart" just in time to ask questions. Rather, we finally get desperate enough to ask and ask until we're up to speed.

It's amazing how hard it can be to ask questions, especially of busy neurologists. We wait weeks to see them and when we finally have their attention, we think our question is trivial or worry about taking too much of their time or go blank and forget what we wanted to ask in the first place.

Write down your questions. And remember, you're the customer! You have the right to ask any and every question and to be treated with respect. If you feel dismissed or hurried, that's a sign that you might want to shop around. The only *right* doctor is one with whom you feel safe, comfortable, and trust to answer all your questions.

Knowledge is empowering. Informed decisions depend on having all the information.

AFFIRMATION: HERE ARE THREE NEW QUESTIONS:

1. _____?

2. _____?

3. _____?

FRIENDSHIP

Family isn't about whose blood you have.
It's about whom you care about.

Trey Parker and Matt Stone, "South Park"

We may create a family of friends because our relatives live far away or because we may not have a healthy, nurturing relationship with them. But whether we choose our friends because of geography, family estrangement, or just because they fulfill different roles than relatives, they are way high up on the MS MUST HAVE list.

I can't begin to describe the value of my friends: Elise drops over to keep me company during my IV drip. Deb distracts me with jokes during botox. Martha prays with me before my MRI.

MS is a great litmus test for discovering who your real friends are. They remember to ask how you're doing even though you look as if you're doing just fine. They show up with food when you're laid up, transportation when needed, love, support, but never pity, knowing full well that's the last thing you'd want. They demonstrate caring and graciously receive your gratitude. They know the six most important words in the English language: What can I do to help?

AFFIRMATION: THANK GOD FOR MY FRIENDS.

REMISSION

One of the most sublime experiences
we can ever have is to wake up feeling
healthy after we have been sick.
Rabbi Harold Kushner

For most people, remissions occur gradually; although there are always exceptions, for the most part symptoms improve slowly and subtly. A leg goes from numb to prickly to so much sensation that we literally pinch ourselves to be sure we aren't imagining things. We have significantly more energy or our vision gets less hazy or our vertigo passes so that the room's no longer spinning.

Remission is usually diagnosed on the basis of a reduction in symptoms, although an MRI or other tests can reinforce our subjective experience. Either way, realizing we're in remission can create a myriad of emotions. We may be scared to get too excited, for fear of being let down or just in case we're imagining things. But for the most part, we're thrilled and grateful, our appreciation of feeling well greatly heightened as a result of having suffered.

Every remission is cause for celebration, offering hope and the prospect of renewed health.

AFFIRMATION: I WILL ENJOY EVERY MOMENT OF IT.

STATISTICS

*USA Today has come out with a new
survey—apparently, three out of every four
people make up 75% of the population.*

David Letterman

I remember shortly after my diagnosis, staring at the computer going down the list of possible MS symptoms, trying to calculate the statistical probability of becoming blind, paralyzed or incontinent, until I started having double vision, my feet were dead asleep and I had to pee so badly it hurt.

They're just numbers and frankly they don't mean a thing unless you happen to pull that particular number. Granted, statistics are a means of gathering information and educating ourselves, but they still must be taken with a large grain of salt, since, again, just because nine out of ten people with MS get drowsy or dizzy from this med or that med, you may still be the exception.

You're not a statistic. You're a human being with MS, an extremely unpredictable disease, all the more reason to be wary of statistics in how you view yourself or choose your treatment plan.

AFFIRMATION: THERE ARE OVER TWO AND A HALF-MILLION PEOPLE IN THE WORLD DIAGNOSED WITH MS. THERE IS ONE ME.

FORGIVENESS

Forgiveness is a gift you give yourself.
Real Live Preacher, RealLivePreacher.com

I'm often asked if I'm angry or bitter over having been misdiagnosed for twenty-five years. There are certain things I'm angry about: The ridiculous sums of time and money spent treating the wrong illness. Devastating depressions. Feeling Crazy. Constant pain. On the other hand, had I been given a diagnosis of MS, who knows what direction my life would have taken? Would I have considered myself an invalid or been cautioned to slow down my pace? Would I have doubted my capacity to pursue my dreams?

I know this much: Nothing was done with malicious intent; mistakes occur, which doesn't put anyone to blame, except perhaps myself for not having pushed harder for answers, and for that, I have forgiven myself.

Real power lies in understanding that the past is the past, moving forward with confidence and serenity.

AFFIRMATION: I WON'T WASTE MY PRECIOUS LIFE ENERGY LOOKING BACKWARD.

DRUGS

Reality is a crutch for people
who can't cope with drugs.

Lily Tomlin

I recently had the privilege of hearing Teri Garr, actress and spokesperson for MSLifelines, speak at a conference. She cracked me up with the line: "Finally, I get to hang out with people who think drugs are good!"

Over twenty percent of the American population are on record as having struggled with some form of substance abuse. If this describes you, you may feel ambivalent about MS meds, but it's critical to make a distinction between recreational drugs and drug therapies that can have a crucial impact on the progression of the disease.

A past history of addiction may make you reticent to pop a pill or fill a syringe, even if just because it triggers memories, good or bad. Please, please, don't let this get in the way of your treatment. Talk to your doctor, your sponsor, and other people in a similar situation. Recovery is recovery. Sometimes it involves drugs.

AFFIRMATION: I'M SECURE IN MY ABILITY TO TREAT MY MS WITHOUT COMPROMISING MY RECOVERY.

EXERCISE

*You have to stay in shape. My grandmother, she
started walking five miles a day when she was 60.
She's 97 today and we don't know where
the hell she is.*

Ellen Degeneres

Unless you live on Mars or some remote island in
the middle of nowhere, stressing the importance of
exercise seems unnecessary given its emphasis in our
culture. But then again, my pathetic little 5 pound
barbells are still sitting in their box from Target and
I've yet to manage the daily walk around the block I
committed to three years ago, so this ones at least
as much for me as for you.

Everyone agrees that exercise should be part of our
overall MS health maintenance program. Working out,
whether walking, running, being on a treadmill, lifting
free weights, dancing, doing aerobics, pilates, yoga,
or even just daily stretching all contribute to keeping
up our strength and improving our overall health and
well-being. We must be careful to not overdo it. But as
long as we're careful, exercise is one of the few ways
to be proactive and improve how we feel. There are so
many benefits. We get a burst of energy plus the added
reward of knowing we're doing something positive to
help ourselves, which makes us feel better all round.

AFFIRMATION: I PROMISE. STARTING TODAY.

RESOURCEFULNESS

If the only tool you have is a hammer,
you tend to see everything as a nail.

Abraham Maslow

Another lesson of living with MS is the opportunity to become more creative. We know what's worked in the past, but now we are charged with new challenges that may require a different set of tools, both on the concrete level and the emotional plane. On the concrete level, we adapt our schedule and find ways to accommodate symptoms and improve both our health and our quality of life, like finding ways to cool down, fitting in naps, taking a yoga class, listening to books on tape, or rearranging our living space.

We may also need to acquire a new or more sophisticated set of emotional coping skills, including patience, acceptance, flexibility, and seeking support from others, which is especially daunting if we're used to handling it all on our own.

We don't have to anymore. Be resourceful in adding new skills—and welcoming new people—into your life.

AFFIRMATION: I AM STRETCHING.

PAIN

Pain is important: how we evade it,
how we succumb to it, how we deal with it,
how we transcend it.

Audre Lorde

If you ask most people to list symptoms of MS, they usually mention fatigue, weakness, numbness, vision problems and difficulties walking. What they don't talk about is pain, which is interesting, since many of us suffer a variety of serious pain syndromes.

Living with MS can involve fleeting pain, recurring pain, sometimes even horrible, unrelenting pain, to the degree that it's excruciating just to be touched. I suffer from Trigeminal Neuralgia, a relatively unusual MS-related syndrome that manifests as searing pain on the right side of my face.

Being in constant pain colors our perceptions, and makes it harder to function, diminishing our quality of life, and destroying our spirit. And yet, we push on, handling it as best we can, hoping and praying for relief.

AFFIRMATION: I LOOK FORWARD TO BEING OUT OF PAIN.

AUTHENTICITY

Do we dare to be ourselves?
This is the question that counts.

Pablo Casals

There is a famous poem by Jenny Joseph called
When I Am Seventy I Will Wear Purple, which begs the
question: Why seventy? If you want to wear purple,
if purple is YOU, why not wear every possible shade
of lilac, lavender and violet, starting right this very
moment? In other words: What are you waiting for?

Each of us is an "original." Part of our task in this
lifetime is to realize our potential by being as totally,
outrageously, authentic as possible. In this journey of
discovery, we come to know ourselves, be ourselves,
love, respect, and celebrate ourselves.

MS can be a catalyst in our commitment to take
bold steps toward expressing and becoming who we
truly are. Ask yourself this question: Is there something
I really want to do? What am I waiting for?

AFFIRMATION: I'M READY TO_____.

PITY

Those who don't complain are never pitied.

Jane Austin

Acceptance, yes. Understanding, absolutely! A dose of sympathy here and there is fine, but the last thing we want is for anyone to feel sorry for us.

People with MS veer toward downplaying discomfort and are extremely sensitive about not being perceived as victims. We may whine or complain or even throw the occasional tantrum, not because we're looking for attention, but because sometimes we just need to vent, which is healthy and normal, as long as we're smart about who's on the receiving end of our rant.

Having one or two people with whom we can let it all out is enormously comforting. Knowing who NOT to complain is equally important. Choosing who we can and can't be vulnerable with is a matter of honor and self-respect.

AFFIRMATION: I DON'T WANT ANYONE'S PITY.

SELF-PITY

Mitch, I don't allow myself any more
self-pity than that. A little each morning,
a few tears, and that's all.

Mitch Albom *Tuesdays with Morrie*

These poignant words from Morrie Schwartz, in the very last stages of Lou Gerhigs Disease, when even taking a breath required inordinate effort.

Repeat: We don't want other peoples' pity. On the other hand, it's perfectly okay to indulge in a little *self-pity*; as long as we don't become overly self-absorbed. Self-pity, in small doses, can open the floodgates and release sadness or anger that may be blocking our ability to function. Being *consumed* with self-pity is a paralyzing cycle that can trigger depression and render us helpless.

Feeling a little sorry for ourselves, once in awhile, a little bit at a time is sometimes all it takes to shift from feeling down to being ready to get up and fight again.

AFFIRMATION: I CAN EXPERIENCE SELF-PITY WITHOUT WALLOWING IN IT.

GENETICS

The apple doesn't fall far from the tree.

Unknown

Although genetics appears to be a relatively minor factor in predicting the likelihood of our children having MS, we still may worry, and rightly so! Statistically, this is more common in females, one reason I panicked when my twenty-two year old daughter, Zoe, began complaining of numbness and tingling.

I hesitated before taking her to a neurologist; I suppose I wasn't ready to reckon with the thought of her having MS. Thankfully, I didn't have to. Her MRI was normal and my fear was alleviated. Had the results been positive, it would still have the right call to have her tested.

It's unnecessary to obsess about passing MS on to our kids, but it's irresponsible to ignore possible warning signs. The statistics are on our side. Both fortunately and unfortunately, we have the experience and knowledge to be especially good parents in the unlikely event that this should come to pass.

AFFIRMATION: I CAN HANDLE IT.

SHOWING UP

I go to Ben's soccer games. And [he]
probably doesn't even stop to think that
I can't see him take a goal. But you know what?
I think kids need you to be there for them.

Richard Cohen

Disability is a poor excuse for checking out and missing out of important occasions, whether it's the school play, a friend's birthday, a family dinner or a community event. Our presence is required. And appreciated, especially when we make the effort despite serious obstacles.

Simply put, its called showing up and it matters! Our kids need to know they can count us to actively participate in what's important to them. Likewise, our friends and relatives feel slighted by our absence, assuming we're not incapacitated, in which case, one would hope they understand.

It isn't easy and *that's* an understatement, but the rewards are abundant. Showing up is a way of letting people know they matter. It's a way of saying: I'm still your mother. Your sister. Your friend.

AFFIRMATION: I'M STILL HERE.

INDIVIDUALITY

*There are exceptions to all
rules—and I am one of them.*

"Forrest Gump"

Most books can't help but generalize to some degree, as in, "most people with MS feel" or "most people with MS discover" and so on and so on. It's assumed that everyone fundamentally shares similar feelings, that most, if not all, people with MS can be expected to act in certain, predictable ways and can be comforted through universal acts of kindness and compassion.

And so I offer this caveat: There are exceptions to all rules, and you may be one of them. Unlike some diseases, MS symptoms vary wildly from person to person; similarly, our experiences run the gamut. Don't allow yourself to be categorized, don't expect yourself to fit anyone's—including my own—description of what its like to live with MS.

Honor your individuality and *insist* on being yourself.

AFFIRMATION: MY EXPERIENCE IS MY EXPERIENCE.

MONEY

You can't pay your American Express
bill with your Visa card.

Unknown

For many people, living with MS means living with less money. A significant percentage of people with MS are currently on disability; even those gainfully employed may struggle with debt, decreased income, expensive health care, and in extreme cases, bankruptcy.

If this doesn't apply to you, thank your lucky stars that you're economically stable and immediately make a contribution, large or small, to the National MS Society. If, however, having MS has caused a financial crisis, here are a few suggestions:

- Do not feel ashamed or embarrassed. Beating yourself up only makes things worse.
- Make an appointment with a financial adviser.
- Get an answering machine or phone messaging so that you don't have to subject yourself to abusive calls from creditors.

Getting support and making a plan are the first important steps toward taking the pressure off and getting your finances in order. It's hard to do, but you'll feel a whole lot better.

AFFIRMATION: I'M TAKING CARE OF BUSINESS.

LABELS

The name we give to something
shapes our attitude toward it.

Katherine Paterson

Crippled. Handicapped. A chronic, debilitating disease for which there is no cure.

The words we choose affect the way we feel. They may even affect the course of our "illness"—yet another loaded word, with negative implications. Even in the MS community there is debate; some people are comfortable with the term MS patients; others prefer MSers. Personally, I don't think of myself as sick, I just think of myself as having MS, just as someone might be have high blood pressure or allergies.

Labels are limiting and can promote stigmatization, which is why, for example, many Deaf people don't consider themselves disabled, but rather, different than those of us who can hear. It may seem like mincing words, but it can mean the difference between feeling less-than and insisting on seeing yourself-and being treated by others-as a normal human being who happens to have this particular challenge to live with.

AFFIRMATION: I PREFER THE TERM _____.

MANIFESTING

I'm thankful for the word Maybe.

Amy Krause Rosenthal

Me, too. Maybe I'll wake up tomorrow feeling rested and energetic. Maybe I won't drop anything or feel weak and shaky or walk into any walls, or _____ (fill in the blank).

Maybe is great. Its one of those "hope" words—and words have a lot of power to convey emotions, describe experience, paint our perceptions, and express our attitudes and beliefs. Some people say we have the capacity to create our experience, a metaphysical idea that may or may not be true. But maybe...............

Try it. Instead of saying: I have MS, I'll never walk again, say out loud: I have MS, maybe some day I'll be able to walk. Maybe my symptoms will go into remission. Maybe I'll get a computer and work from home.

Manifest it and maybe it will come to pass.

AFFIRMATION: MAYBE _____.

GUILT

I'm sorry.

Parents with MS

Like every other parent, we feel guilty when we let our children down. We love them so much and want to be able to give them everything we've got. But sometimes, "everything" doesn't feel like enough, as we grapple with the gap between our image of the "perfect parent' and the limitations of living with MS.

I wish I had a dollar for every time I had to tell my children, "Mommy's sick. I can't go on the field trip." Now that they're in college, I still feel awful when fatigue or pain prevents me from being there for them.

How do we reconcile the gap? By knowing that we're doing our best. By remembering that our kids may be resentful or judgmental, especially once they're teenagers, but no more so than any other kids whose parents don't have MS. Chances are, we're hardest on ourselves. There's every reason to believe that our kids will turn out fine.

AFFIRMATION: I LOVE MY CHILDREN MORE THAN THEY WILL EVER KNOW.

SELF-PLEASURE

Don't knock masturbation.
It's sex with someone I love.

Woody Allen

Sexual dysfunction, another common MS symptom, needn't mean abstinence. Whether we are or aren't in an intimate relationship, whether we're tired, feeling lousy, or just not at the top of our game, it's still essential to nurture our sexuality.

There are lots of ways to touch and be touched: Hugs from friends. Body massage. Long, sensual baths with music, incense and candles are all ways to relax and get in touch with our eroticism.

Masturbation is another, perfectly healthy way to experience our sexuality. It feels good, and its good for us. Make time to take pleasure in your body, in any way that feels delicious, as often as you wish.

AFFIRMATION: Mmmmmmm.........Ahhhhhhhh........

ACCEPTANCE

I never ask, Why me? because
then I'd have to ask, Why me? for all
the great things in my life.

Arthur Ashe

This comment from one of tennis's greats, Arthur Ashe, was shared just months before his death from AIDs. He speaks to each of us struggling with the question: Why me? Why was I chosen to have MS?

But, as Ashe points out, if we question our ill fortune, then we must equally question all the wonderful gifts we've been given and continue to receive: Why have I enjoyed such success in my career? Why have I been given such terrific children? Why have I been granted a group of such loving friends and family whom I can depend on to be there when I need them?

Perhaps there's no answer to the question why? but rather, an equal acceptance of the good with the bad.

AFFIRMATION: BECAUSE

GIVING

Giving is the only flight in space
permitted to human beings.

Anais Nin

Reciprocity is a fundamental part of friendship, and giving feels good, whether to strangers in need or to our nearest and dearest. When we're feeling down, it can be extremely comforting to extend kindness to others. There are countless ways to give: By volunteering at a shelter, soup kitchen or nursing home. By signing up to be a Big Sister or Big Brother, collecting for a charity, or reaching out to someone else who has MS or another chronic condition.

Being sick is hard enough, without feeling needy and useless. In times of distress, our loved ones can be excessively kind and caring. The only catch comes when they stop asking for *our* help-and when we stop believing that we're needed.

In helping someone else, we realize how much we really have. And, how much we have to give.

AFFIRMATION: GIVE OF YOURSELF AND EMBRACE THE GRACE OF OTHERS.

DREAMING

It's good to pay attention to your dreams.

Natalie Goldberg

Our dreams are an expression of the deepest level of our psyche, and, they provide useful information through imagery and symbols.

Suzanne, a recently divorced woman with MS, related her dream: "I was in a dark cave. Bats were flying all around. I screamed, but the sound echoed and no one came. Suddenly I saw a lantern... I crawled toward it and when I reached the light, I saw my mother's hands."

Suzanne awakened from her dream, tears streaming down her face. She discovered, much to her surprise, that she needed her mother, whom she had been estranged from for years, and who she proceeded to welcome back into her life.

Think of dreams as messengers offering you insight. Write them down and notice what they tell you about yourself.

AFFIRMATION: LAST NIGHT I DREAMED..............

WISDOM

And to all the voices of wisdom that
whispered to me along the way....

Dhyani Ywahoo

I give thanks.

These words sound like a prayer. And a gentle reminder to heed the voices of wisdom that offer comfort and solace.

There are so many ways to listen. One way is to keep a list of all the helpful advice we've gathered from friends and others in the MS community (there's lots more available on MS internet websites). We can surround ourselves with inspiring quotes, tape them on our mirror or refrigerator, immerse ourselves in inspirational books, music or seminars, or attend worship services and study spiritual texts that speak to our hearts.

I once heard Oprah Winfrey describe God as "a whisper in her ear." What are some of the voices of wisdom whispering to you? What do you hear?

AFFIRMATION. THE BEST PIECE OF WISDOM I'VE BEEN GIVEN IS..............

BREATHING

I wear my lungs like a pair of water wings
To keep me afloat in my breath.

Miriam Sagan

When we're anxious and upset our breathing gets shallow and quick, as if we're fighting to stay afloat. Yoga, meditation, biofeedback, and other methods of relaxation can help us stay centered and calm.

We can commit to a formal discipline, setting aside time each day for mediation. Or, we can simply pay attention to our breathing—in and out—inhale, exhale, slow and easy.

When we feel anxious, it helps to stop, close our eyes for a moment, and breathe. Just breathe. It's the basis of life, a natural way to restore serenity and peace.

AFFIRMATION: MY BODY BREATHES ITSELF.

GOALS

To have a reason to get up in the morning,
it's necessary to possess a guiding principle.

Judith Guest

Some days it's really hard to get up and get going, when just putting one foot in front of the other feels like an Olympic feat.

It helps to have a guiding principle. It may be expressed as a tangible goal: Today I'll finish all the work on my desk (better yet, half the work on my desk) or, This week I will make a point of drinking at least four glasses of water a day.

It also may be expressed as a bedrock belief, which, if we follow, motivates and focuses us, for example: "I'm willing to trust the Universe." or "One day at a time."

When you feel overwhelmed, dispirited, or just too tired to pull yourself out of bed, what do you think or feel or say to yourself in order to get up and get through the day?

AFFIRMATION: TODAY MY GUIDING PRINCIPLE IS:

NATURE

When I'm out in nature, I feel whole, peaceful,
at one with everything around me.

Jeanne Engelman

Being close to nature replenishes our energy and nourishes our soul. We breathe in the brisk air, awed by the gloriously changing colors of autumn leaves. Spring turns to summer as we swim in the river or bathe in the sunshine (not too long!!). We're moved by the majesty of mountains in the distance, inspired by the ocean, a faint outline, which reaches into infinity.

Nature is healing. Make time, even if its only a few minutes each day, to be outdoors. Every reunion with nature, whether it's a short walk or a week in the wilderness, makes us feel more whole, more alive, and more attuned to all that is holy.

AFFIRMATION. NATURE IS NURTURING.
TODAY I WILL MAKE TO BE OUTDOORS.

HUMAN SPIRIT

*Man never made any material
as resilient as the human spirit.*

Bern Williams

Witness the courage of individuals with terminal illness weathering chemotherapy, struggling to survive, despite overwhelming odds. Or the emotional fortitude displayed by victims of natural disasters like the Tsunami earthquake, searching for missing friends and relatives, picking through piles of rubble, resolutely rebuilding their homes.

So too, those of us with MS can depend on our inner strength to see us through. The hard times are hard, there's no way around it. But we can count on a vast inner store of resolve and resiliency to get us through even the worst of times, especially when we're in pain or in the midst of a relapse.

We know we are bouncing back when our concentration improves, when we can think about something other than our symptoms. When we're less edgy, more patient, and people quit walking on eggshells around us. When we wake up one morning and realize we're smiling and looking forward to the day,

AFFIRMATION: FINALLY!!

TRANSFORMATION

Perhaps all the dragons in our lives are
princesses who are only waiting to see us act,
just once, with beauty and courage.

Rainer Maria Rilke

When bad things happen, we're apt to feel angry and resentful and wonder why they're happening to us. But what it, as the poet Rilke suggests, the bad things are actually good things? What if the absolute hardest times are actually the best times in life? What if the proverbial "dragons" are princesses in disguise, golden opportunities to act with beauty and courage?

In this way, we grow through MS. Think of a moment, an incident related to having MS when you've conducted yourself with dignity and grace. When you've risen to the challenge. When you've felt incredibly proud of yourself for how you've coped with setbacks, new symptoms, physical or emotional challenges that have taken everything you've got.

What inner pool of strength did you tap in order to transform a negative into a positive?

AFFIRMATION: I ROSE TO THE OCCASION WHEN I ____

_____.

TIMING

Time is nature's way of preventing
everything from happening at once.

Graffiti

In the present we may feel overwhelmed; but in
retrospect, we realize we can trust our innate sense
of good timing. When we were ready to see
a medical provider, we did. When we were ready to
start treatment, we did. When we were ready to tell
our family, we did. When we were ready to ask for
their help and support, we did.

We needn't take on everything at once; it's taken
me two and a half years to apply for a handicapped-
parking sticker and I'm still waffling on attending a
support group. Unquestionably, its critical to seek
diagnoses and begin treatment as soon as possible, the
rest can be dealt with in our own good time. Whether
attending a support group, exploring legal and financial
resources, or going on the Internet to get the most up
to date information on MS research, trust your own
timing. You're ready when you're ready and that's
plenty soon enough.

AFFIRMATION: THERE'S NO RUSH.

JOURNAL WRITING

All sorrows can be borne
if you put them into a story.

Isak Dinesen

Here's my plug for keeping a journal—not just about our losses and limitations, but about every part of our experience, the joys and the sorrows, what makes us laugh and what makes us cry.

Telling our story, by writing in a journal or sharing our experience with someone we trust, makes for a richer, more meaningful existence. It also makes it easier to live with MS. Giving words to our experience makes it more real, more tangible, easier to wrap our minds around. It's a way to maintain a daily commitment to record what's happening right now, as well as something to look back on over time.

Writing is a wonderful creative outlet; so are painting, making music, baking a cake or building a cabin. If you choose to write in a journal, here's how to start: Open the first page of a an empty notebook or a new screen on your computer and begin with this sentence:

AFFIRMATION: AT THIS VERY MOMENT I AM FEELING _

GOOD JUDGMENT

*This thing that we call 'failure' is not the
falling down, but the staying down.*

Mary Pickford.

I'm on the phone talking to Laura, a woman in
Connecticut whose main MS symptoms are blurred
vision and vertigo. "I'm getting better," she confides,
"I'm working up the courage to ride my bike around
the block."

Back to first grade! For Laura, whose MS was
diagnosed after suffering a concussion from falling off
her bike, getting back on the horse—or in her case,
the bike—is a risky endeavor. She may ride like a pro;
she may fall again and decide that for now, at least,
walking is safer.

The operative word is "decide." Using good
judgment—deciding if, when, and how to resume some
of our pre-MS activities—is yet another MS survival
tool. Consult your medical provider and use your
common sense, which may tell you this is or isn't the
right time, or, that certain activities may need to be
tabled or replaced by others to accommodate your
needs. You be the judge. There's no way to fail if
you're willing to keep figuring it out as you go.

AFFIRMATION: BE CAREFUL

COMMUNITY

When you are in this disease or any chronic disease, it's all of us. There is nobody different, really. It is just the symptoms that are different. But other than that, we are all in the same boat.

David (Sqiggy) Lander

In a recent counseling session with Sara, a woman newly diagnosed with MS, I was struck once again by how difficult circumstances can be fertile opportunities for growth. A long history of abuse had kept Sara isolated; she had few friends and was extremely mistrustful. Within a week of her diagnosis and with a little bit of nudging, she registered for an MS support group, signed up for a walkathon, attended a seminar on how to apply for disability, while calling me regularly to let me know how she was doing. I told her, both genuinely and jokingly, If you have to have something, it might as well be MS, because you were just awarded membership in one of the best clubs around.

The MS community is a global network filled with caring and knowledgeable people of every color, culture, and background, sharing experience and supporting one another. I would never have chosen to have MS. That said, I couldn't hope to be in better company.

AFFIRMATION: WE'RE ALL IN THIS TOGETHER.

FLOWERS

Won't you come into my garden?
My roses would like to see you.

Richard B. Sheridan

If you indulge in one area, make it flowers. A bouquet of fresh tulips, delicate roses, or breathtaking irises is one sure way to pamper yourself and brighten your spirits.

Planting a garden also yields plentiful rewards. We put on our oldest, most comfortable clothes, dig in the dirt, participate in creation, and sow seeds for the future. Besides, gardening is a lovely way to pass time in solitude, to tune in to ourselves without pressure to converse, without feeling as if we *ought* to be anywhere else.

And so we water our tomatoes, talk—and listen—to our roses, plant our perennials, and, perhaps shed a few tears in the privacy of our garden, reconnecting to life, to hope, to nature in all her majesty.

AFFIRMATION: I WILL SURROUND MYSELF WITH NATURE'S BOUNTY.

COMFORT

There's no place like home.

Dorothy, The Wizard of Oz

Creating the right environment takes on greater importance when we have MS, especially for those of us who live in very hot or very cold climates and need to spend a fair share of time indoors. If we're housebound we want our home to not only be handicapped accessible, but cozy and comfortable. We may also spend more time at home due to fatigue, bouts of depression, lack of mobility, or other MS symptoms that can make going out such a major production that sometimes, its just easier to stay home.

Since fatigue is one of those almost universal MS symptoms, having a peaceful place to rest, be it the bedroom, living room couch or our favorite recliner, is a real priority. Having a comfortable place increases feelings of security and serenity, as long as we don't get SO comfortable that we become a recluse. As long as we remember that there's a whole world waiting right outside our door.

AFFIRMATION: I CAN CREATE A NURTURING ENVIRONMENT

Words of Inspiration For People with MS

PURPOSE

One thing life teaches you is, life is short. I want to stand for something.

Neil Cavuto, news anchor

Another MS lesson is the heightened awareness of our mortality. How we live and what we stand for isn't a philosophical question, but rather, a matter of urgency, something to carefully ponder. We realize that life is capricious and nothing should be taken for granted. Relapses can come at any moment, there's no absolute way to predict and prepare for the future, so now is the time to act.

More than ever before, carpe diem, the Latin expression for "seize the moment" rings true, as does our motivation to ask ourselves these questions: What do I stand for? Does my life have meaning? Am I making a difference in the lives of others, be it simple or spectacular, so that when my time on Earth is over, I will truly be able to know:

AFFIRMATION: THIS IS WHAT I STOOD FOR.

PERCEPTIONS

*We must not allow other peoples
limited perceptions to define us.*

Virginia Satir

My seventy seven year old mother is an ovarian cancer survivor. Twenty years ago, immediately following surgery, an oncologist waltzed into her hospital room and made the following pronouncement: "You have two years, or less, to live," sounding her death knell to my dad, sister, myself and my mom still swimming her way through the daze of anesthesia.

The same scenario comes into play for people with MS. Being told we have an incurable disease or being given an unnecessarily pessimistic prognosis can mess with our motivation to take good care of ourselves and take advantage of treatment options. Limited perceptions are just that—limited; they don't account for individual determination, scientific breakthroughs, or unexplained turnarounds that defy medical explanation.

The best way to override damaging or limiting perceptions, such as the assumption that all people with MS end up in wheelchairs or that pregnancy causes too high a risk for someone with MS, is to be confident in our own knowledge of what's true and what's reasonable to expect—including miracles, which happen every day.

AFFIRMATION: I TRUST MY INSTINCTS.

SURVIVAL

If you were healed of a dreadful wound,
you did not want to keep the bandage.

Ursula Reilly Curtiss

It would seem reasonable to want to forget about the times when our MS has been the most difficult to bear. For me, it was probably a few months after being diagnosed, when I fell out of bed and broke my collarbone in the middle of the night while taking a medication that made me dizzy and disoriented.

But there's something to be said for "keeping our bandages"—the tangible or symbolic remnants that remind us of what we've been through: The cards we've kept from the people who care about us. Photographs of ourselves, puffy from prednisone. The ragged, cotton sling, stuffed in my drawer that brings back memories of the pain I was in, how helpless I felt, and how grateful I was when my friend, Nate, stopped by, at least once a day, to see if there was anything I needed.

These artifacts provide powerful testimony to all we've overcome, while reminding us to appreciate and savor what its like to feel better, as long as it lasts.

AFFIRMATION: I HONOR MY MEMORIES AS PERSONAL BADGES OF COURAGE.

INFORMATION

You know doctors. For every one
thing they tell you, there are two things
hidden under their tongue.

Rose Chernin

Some people only want to know what they need to know. Others, myself included, want every single solitary piece of information, not just a detailed explanation of every test and its results, but what the results imply in terms of predicting how certain symptoms might progress, whether my neurologist thinks the almost imperceptible lag in my right leg means anything, his opinion regarding new treatments on the horizon, and, since I happen to be in his office, would he mind taking a quick look at the mole on my left arm? Enough is enough!

A trusting relationship with a doctor who is thorough, respectful, and responsible is essential. Obsessing, catastrophizing or getting paranoid that your doctor is hiding something is excessive. If you need more information, say so. Don't expect your doctor to be an oracle or an encyclopedia. Do expect your doctor to give you a reasonable degree of attention and time.

AFFIRMATION: I WILL SEEK AS MUCH INFORMATION AS IS NEEDED, WITHIN REASON.

INSPIRATION

He reached into that enormous and beautiful
and generous heart of his and gave us his life.
We can at the very least try to do the same

Dana Reeve

Actor and activist Christopher Reeve died on
October 10th, 2004. He spent the last third of his life
as a quadriplegic, paralyzed from the neck down from
a riding accident. He used that time to create the
Christopher Reeve Foundation, fighting for the rights
of people with disabilities and raising money for
research, including a substantial grant to help
find a cure for MS.

Ironically, he was best known for his role as Superman.
In the last year and a half of his life, Reeve produced
and directed a made for TV movie about the life of
Brooke Ellison, a twenty-six year old quadriplegic, who
graduated form Harvard, Summa Cum Laude. In his last
interview, he talked about why the film had been so
important for him to make: "I wanted to offer a message
of compassion and being able to imagine what it's like
to be somebody else. If that can get through, then we've
really accomplished something," he said.

We honor his memory with his lasting words:
We can. We will. We must.

AFFIRMATION: MAY HE REST IN PEACE.

AND MORE INSPIRATION

My experiences, both inside and outside
the classroom have been with one goal in mind:
helping to empower those who face adversity
or discouragement of any kind.

Brooke Ellison,

Brooke Ellison, the subject of Christopher Reeve's last artistic endeavor, based on her memoir, The Brooke Ellison Story: One Mother. One Daughter. One Journey, deserves her own page in this book.

In a riveting interview with Larry King, it was impossible to imagine what it must be like for this brilliant young woman to be trapped in a useless shell of a body, propped in a supremely equipped wheelchair with so many bells and whistles it almost looked like a car.

Yet there she was; poised, candid, and optimistic, without the slightest hint of self-pity despite being a quadriplegic since age eleven, the result of a car accident. When asked about her plans for the future, she shared her dreams of politics or academia. When asked whether spirituality or religion were part of what keeps her going, Ellison paused and then said what perhaps is the most important thing for those of us living with MS or any other disability. She said: "My faith is love."

AFFIRMATION: LOVE IS THE MOST POWERFUL FORCE IN THE UNIVERSE.

CLICHES

*The clichés of a culture sometimes
tell the deepest truths.*

Faith Popcorn

We dismiss and resent when people offer up clichés as
a form of reassurance: This, too, shall pass. Suffering
builds character. It's always darkest before dawn. Of
course, the reason they're clichés is because they're
true! We dismiss them as cheap, simplistic Hallmark
sayings, when, in fact, the reason they've lingered in
our vernacular is because they contain wisdom that's
held up over time.

Think about it: *This, too, shall pass.* Now recall
your initial reaction to being diagnosed with MS and
reflect upon how, with time, the shock has dissipated.
Suffering builds character. Consider one way in which
living with MS has been difficult to endure, then think
about how you have grown stronger as a result.
It's always darkest before the dawn: Recall your
darkest moment, perhaps even an instance of despair
so intense you considered suicide, and then notice
how once the incident passed, you regained the
capacity for happiness and joy.

Here's one particular cliché that I find
deeply comforting:

AFFIRMATION: EVERYTHING HAPPENS FOR A REASON.
(turn the page to find out why.)

DESTINY

At any rate, I am convinced that
God does not play dice with the Universe.

Albert Einstein

It takes a great deal of faith to believe that everything is happening as it should, especially when what's happening definitely wasn't part of our plans, much less something we're thankful for.

Yet, the belief in a purposeful universe is shared by many, and makes sense on a number of levels. For example, how do we account for so-called coincidences? And, why, in retrospect, do seemingly arbitrary occurrences turn out to be synchronistic, life-changing experiences? Why do "bad things happen to good people?" Is life truly random or does "every snowflake fall in exactly the right place?"

It doesn't matter. What matters is whether what we believe in enables us to feel more peaceful and empowered in our day-to-day lives. Whether or not we believe that things happen for a reason, this much is true. What we're given is our fate. What we do with it is our destiny.

AFFIRMATION: LIFE IS A LEAP OF FAITH

MYSTERY

*Not only does God play dice with the
Universe, he sometimes throws them
where they cannot be seen.*

Stephen W. Hawking

Einstein proposes that things happen for a reason;
world famous physicist, Stephen Hawking reminds
us that it isn't always easy to understand why.

The search for answers can be intriguing, as long
as we don't get bogged down in intellectual debate.
Asking why I am ambulatory when so many people
with MS are in wheelchairs is a fair question, but even
if there was a good answer, it wouldn't change a thing.
Wondering if something could have been done to
prevent our having MS, or worse, if we could have
done something that caused it, is an exercise in futility,
except as a subject of research that can potentially
impact the ifs and the whys.

For now, we accept that life is mysterious. We don't
have all the answers. Perhaps we're not meant to.

AFFIRMATION: I EMBRACE THE MYSTERY

DETERMINATION

You may be disappointed if you fail,
but you are doomed if you don't try.

Beverly Sills

Legendary opera diva and long-time MS advocate and fundraiser, Beverly Sills, can attest to the phenomenal effort required to live an extraordinary life. Or, as the old joke goes: Q: How do you get to Carnegie Hall? A: Practice!

There are times when we just can't summon the energy to keep overcoming obstacles. We get tired and discouraged. We lose confidence in our ability to go the extra mile.

We do it because we have to. Because we have bills to pay and kids to raise—because tomorrow is another day and because we know, deep down, that it's better to fight than fold. We are fighters, my friends, each and every one of us—and we're determined to win.

Ultimately, giving it a shot feels better than giving up. When we feel like giving up, we need to take a break and rest for a while. Rested and replenished, we try again. And again.

AFFIRMATION: I CAN DO IT!

EFFORT

I am so very tired sometimes of trying.
I'm trying all the time.

Ann, *Exposure*

Here's the other side: Living with MS takes an incredible amount of energy. We get tired of trying to be positive and hopeful. We get tired of feeling tired, of trying to juggle so many responsibilities, handling work pressure, financial pressure, and family pressure when we wish we could just crawl under the covers and disappear.

So what do we do when we're tired? We give ourselves a little slack. We rest, let down, and give ourselves permission to stop trying for a while. It's hard to stop; it feels like giving up and it doesn't permanently solve the problem of having far too much to do, with too little energy.

It's so frustrating to try so hard and never feel like its enough. Right now it's time to rest and recharge our batteries. Tomorrow we can take a serious look at our priorities and explore creative ways to lessen our load, as well as our guilt!

AFFIRMATION: RIGHT NOW I DON'T HAVE TO TRY.
I JUST GET TO BE.

REGRET

If only one could have two lives:
the first in which to make one's mistakes…..
and the second in which to profit by them.

D.H.Laurence

We may be plagued by regret: over mistakes made, opportunities missed, things we wish we had done before having MS imposed certain limitations on our lives.

That was then. This is now. Many religions embrace the idea of reincarnation—that we keep coming back over many different lifetimes in many different forms in order to "work out our karma."

Whether we're here once or several times around, regret is a senseless waste of time and energy. So what if we never learned how to ski or we didn't make it to the Grand Canyon, or we weren't always sympathetic when friends of ours were ill.

Regret is paralyzing. Action is liberating. We make amends for the past, learn from our mistakes and do our best to live honorably, making sure to take advantage of all that lies ahead.

AFFIRMATION: I PUT THE PAST BEHIND ME AS I CREATE THE FUTURE.

SUCCESS

My private measure of success is daily.
If this were to be the last day of my life
would I be content with it?

Jane Rule

How we measure success is subjective. And constantly evolving. Some of the things we used to do may not be an option anymore, like putting in overtime or going snow-boarding or making pumpkin pie from scratch and having the whole family over for Thanksgiving dinner. Some days we may feel relatively motivated and energetic, other days it takes monumental effort to make it through the ten o'clock news.

What really determines success is how we feel about who we are and what we're accomplishing. What have you done today that you feel good about? If this were, indeed, the last day of your life, what would it take for you to be able to say:

AFFIRMATION: I AM CONTENT.

PERSPECTIVE

Angels can fly because they
take themselves lightly

GK Chesterton

It's an interesting paradox: How to take our MS seriously, while simultaneously remembering that, in the great scheme of things, it's not that big a deal.

Things could be worse. Or better. Or, different. Keeping things in perspective means seeing the big picture, staying calm, making sure to be aware of both the difficulties and the rewards, even being able to laugh at ourselves every once in a while.

Having spent time getting to know lots of people who have MS, the ones who fare the best seem to share these two qualities: The capacity to see humor in even the most humiliating and exasperating circumstances. And, a conscious commitment to take responsibility for their health and well-being.

Being overly dramatic weighs us down. Keeping it light helps us stay afloat.

AFFIRMATION: LIGHTEN UP

INTIMACY

I wanted him to understand that if I said
I was tired, it's because I really was, and not
because I didn't want to see him.

A woman on an MS website

How grateful we are to have a loving, supportive partner. Still, at times it feels like a mixed blessing. We know he wants the best for us, but we hate how he hovers. We've given her all the information to read and she *still* asks us to explain the difference between relapse remitting and primary progressive. He says he understands when we'd rather sleep than have sex, but the underlying tension makes us anxious that, sooner or later, he'll turn to someone else.

Some of our fears can be relieved with open, honest conversation with our partner. Others are imaginary, born of fear, reinforced by the belief that having MS makes us less appealing, a burden, maybe even "damaged goods."

Our partners can reassure us, up to a point. Beyond that, we're responsible for finding ways to strengthen our self-esteem and keep believing:

AFFIRMATION: I AM EVERY BIT AS DESIRABLE AS I WAS BEFORE I HAD MS.

AMAZING CAREPARTNERS

As we took our vows on a beautiful beach
in Kauai, I was overwhelmed with the love
and acceptance of this beautiful man. I didn't
have a choice to live with MS, he did.

Kari Bertch

Challenges aside, I am constantly amazed by the extraordinary level of love and devotion I see in most couples living with MS.

Bob and Nancy Schiff are members of the temple where I worship. Every time I see them together I'm moved by his passionate commitment to go the distance in supporting her. Nancy walks with a cane; Bob is never more than six steps away from her. He goes to her doctor appointments and is up on the latest medical developments. Several years ago he put in a swimming pool so she can exercise, and, he captains "Nancy's Team" which raises substantial money as part of their local NMSS chapter MS walk.

Living with MS gives new meaning to "for better and for worse." Sometimes the worst brings out the best, and for that we say:

AFFIRMATION: THANK YOU

ANXIETY

Don't get scared in advance.

Cindy Bloomquist

This simple piece of advice got me through the first weeks after being diagnosed with MS. They came from Cindy Bloomquist, a woman I met years ago when our daughters were in kindergarten. She had four children, worked as a physicist, and seemed to have infinite energy, along with a fabulous attitude. I'd heard through the grapevine that she had MS. She was so positive and matter of fact about it that that ten years later, I called her, knowing she'd be just the right person to talk to when my vivid imagination took me to some very scary places.

What she said is simple. And true. Don't get scared in advance. I've written these words on a Postit note tucked inside my wallet. I offer them to you as a reminder to stay focused on what is, rather than worrying about what might be.

AFFIRMATION: I WON'T GET AHEAD OF MYSELF.

ATTITUDE

*Each of us is singularly
responsible for our attitude.*

Victor Frankl

These words from Holocaust survivor, Victor Frankl's, memoir, *Man's Search for Meaning*, go way beyond the concept of having a positive attitude, one of those slogans that's so overused its almost lost its power to inspire, kind of like those smiley faces people put on the bottom of their e-mails.

Yet, when all is said and done, attitude is one of the few, if only, things we actually have control over (and if that doesn't work, there's always antidepressants.) But seriously, having a positive attitude doesn't mean pretending to be happy all the time. It means feeling what we're feeling, be it anger, sadness, fear, or joy, and then summoning our best energy to get to the other side.

AFFIRMATION: I HAVE ENORMOUS POWER TO CREATE A POSITIVE MINDSET.

MASQUERADE

When one is pretending
the entire body revolts.

Anais Nin

It takes effort to maintain a façade. When our children need our attention, we may force ourselves to look cheerful. We may pretend too be interested in our partner even though we're in pain. We put our best face forward in the workplace; there may be one or two colleagues we confide in, but for the most part, we try to appear as healthy and "normal" as possible.

The same is true for social occasions, one reason why we may decline invitations or avoid being in public when we're feeling particularly vulnerable. We don't want to be a drag, but we also don't want to put on an act.

Which poses the dilemma: What do we say when someone asks: How are you? Do we keep it simple and say: "Fine" or, do we say, "Well, if you really want to know................" only applies to your nearest and dearest, and, trust me, sometimes even they prefer the cliff notes.

Be discerning. Sometimes its worth it to be "real"-other times it makes sense to temporarily keep up appearances.

AFFIRMATION: IT'S OKAY TO PRETEND I'M FEELING BETTER THAN I AM

JOY

May your walls know joy;
May every room hold laughter and every
window open to great possibility.

Maryanne Radmacher-Hershey

I know lots of people with MS and I can honestly say, our collective joy is far greater than any overriding sense of misery. Joy seems to be a byproduct of shared support. Or maybe once we reconcile ourselves to having MS, we're freed to savor life in a whole new way.

Perhaps our joy quotient increases as a result of having endured so much pain. Plus, its amazingly inspiring to belong to a community of people who are committed to making the best of difficult circumstances, who understand that its up to us to create joy in our lives. In the walls of our homes, in the rooms of our lives, lighting a candle of hope that's a beacon to all people everywhere. Let it be known: Our lives may not be easy. But they are divine.

AFFIRMATION: I AM OVERFLOWING.

SURRENDER

Life is a rock. And a hard place.

Juli Duncan

And what about of those times when it just plain sucks? When there's no obvious solution? When it seems as if we've exhausted every strategy and still feel stuck?

Then we need to shift gears, from the urgency of trying to figure out the right answer to the serenity of accepting that for now, at least, it's time to surrender. Surrender has nothing to do with giving up, but rather giving us time to regroup. It can also involve "giving ourselves over" spiritually, by seeking solace and sustenance from God, Buddha, Krishna, Allah, or any other higher power.

When we're able to detach and get a little distance from our immediate frustration, eventually we remember again that we have choices. Sometimes the choice is to wait. And sometimes we need to act. The first step is to think of another time when you felt at the end of your rope and then say out loud:

AFFIRMATION: I'VE BEEN HERE BEFORE. HERE'S WHAT I DID:

PERFECTIONISM

I dreamed my whole house was clean
Inscribed on my favorite mug

...but then I awoke to a sinkful of dirty dishes, including this cup, which reminds me to chill out and accept the fact that try as I might, there's no way to get everything done, yet another daily lesson of living with MS.

Creating realistic expectations is a dynamic process that requires cultivating flexibility, perspective, self-acceptance and the capacity to constantly adjust our priorities according to our health. Some days we've got tons of energy and check off everything on our list. The next day we may tank, but if we let that get to us, we feel disappointed and bummed out.

Its frustrating to live with a watered down version of what we're capable of doing. It can also be freeing, once we understand that we're not lowering our expectations, we're simply honing in on what's truly important so we can maximize our energy and feel good about what we are accomplishing.

AFFIRMATION: I'll MAKE A SHORTER LIST

APPRECIATION

There are never enough "I love you's".
Lenny Bruce

The 911 terrorist attack on the World Trade Center was a wake up call, not just in terms of national security, but also on a more personal level, making us acutely aware of how important it is to acknowledge and appreciate one-another, not just in the midst of crisis, but every single day.

Adversity can kick start gratitude, pain can be a potent incentive to be more open in expressing our love. This was brought home to me a few years ago while speaking at a National MS Society annual conference. Frankly, the idea of spending a weekend with so many "suffering" people seemed a little depressing, at best. In fact, it was practically a love fest. I can't recall another instance in my life when I've been surrounded by so many people offering encouragement, support, and yes, love.

Yet another silver lining of living with MS. It may seem like a little thing, but saying "I love you," matters hugely and is immeasurably healing.

AFFIRMATION: I AM SO, SO GRATEFUL FOR THE LOVE IN MY LIFE.

FLEXIBILITY

Dare to dream big, but be prepared
to change the plan on a dime.

Ellen Sue Stern

One of the most predictable things about MS is its unpredictability, which puts us in the interesting and infuriating position of figuring out how to plan anything when we don't know how we're going to feel from one moment to the next.

The choice is ours. We can choose to live small, protecting ourselves by scaling back our expectations. Or, we can paint our lives on a large canvass, as long as we don't get overly attached to how the picture looks.

My favorite refrigerator magnet (which is rarely on my refrigerator because I like to have it with me all the time) reads: Nothing is too good to be true. In short, there's nothing keeping you or me or anyone else, regardless of MS or any serious challenge, from aiming high and reaching far. We may have physical limitations, and, sure there are days when our minds are a little muddled, but nothing—nothing- can get in the way of our dreams

AFFIRMATION: EVERYTHING IS POSSIBLE.

MIRACLES

She would consider each day a miracle—which indeed it is, when you consider the number of unexpected things that could happen in each second of our fragile existences.

Paolo Coelho

We are fragile. And miraculous. In the empowering words of my friend and musician, Kristy Salerno Kent, we are "Mighty Souls"—every single one of us.

Every morning, when we awaken and greet the day with optimism is a miracle. Every time we face barriers with bravery is a miracle. Every loving gesture, every stubborn refusal to fold, every time we reach deep within to tap our inner source of strength and creativity is a miracle and a testament to the potential for greatness inherent in humanity.

Our lives are sacred—each sunrise brings the chance to discover the unknown, to welcome today and tomorrow and tomorrow....

AFFIRMATION: I WILL MAKE MY LIFE A BLESSING.

INFINITY

May you build a ladder to the stars
and climb up every rung.

Bob Dylan

...and may you stay healthy and hopeful and grateful
and courageous and confident and loving and proud of
who you are and how you continue to walk this path
with an open mind and a gentle heart.

AFFIRMATION: AND MAY YOU STAY, FOREVER YOUNG.

BOOKS BY ELLEN SUE STERN